Julia Castle Builder

by Dana Lynch

SCHOOL PUBLISHERS

Cover, ©Craig Aurness/Hearst Castle/CA Park Service/Corbis; p.3, p.6, ©Environmental Design Archives/Online Archives of California; p.4, p.5, p.7, ©Library of Congress Prints & Photographs Division; p.8, ©Historic Photo Archive/Getty Images; p.9, ©Bancroft Library/Online Archives of California; p.10, ©Hulton Archive/Getty Images; p.11, ©Expuesto-Nicolas Randall/Alamy; p.12, ©Reed Saxon/ AP Images; p.13, ©Environmental Designs Archives/Online Archives of California; The Bancroft Library/University of California, Berkeley/Online Archives of California; p.14, ©Chuck Pefley/Alamy.

Requests for permission to make copies of any part of the work should be addressed to School Permissions and Copyrights, Harcourt, Inc., 6277 Sea Harbor Drive, Orlando, Florida 32887-6777. Fax: 407-345-2418.

HARCOURT and the Harcourt Logo are trademarks of Harcourt, Inc., registered in the United States of America and/or other jurisdictions.

Printed in China

ISBN 10: 0-15-350453-6
ISBN 13: 978-0-15-350453-2

Ordering Options
ISBN 10: 0-15-350333-5 (Grade 3 Below-Level Collection)
ISBN 13: 978-0-15-350333-7 (Grade 3 Below-Level Collection)
ISBN 10: 0-15-357464-X (package of 5)
ISBN 13: 978-0-15-357464-1 (package of 5)

4 5 6 7 8 9 10 0940 12 11 10 09

Julia's Way

The young woman shook her head. She tore away the tiles. The workers stared. They didn't expect women to get their hands dirty. She showed them the tiles. They were scratched. They were not good enough. Julia Morgan's buildings had to be the best.

Julia Morgan was born in 1872. Her family lived in Oakland, California. She had three brothers and one sister.

Julia liked math and science. She liked doing research to find out about things.

Julia finished high school in 1890. Then she wanted to go to college.

Oakland, California

University of California, Berkeley

Most women did not go to college.
Julia's family did not want her to
be disappointed. They said that she
could go to college. She was smart
and talented. She worked hard. The
University of California, Berkeley, was
nearby. Julia would go there.

A drawing by Julia Morgan

Learning How

Julia studied to be an engineer. Engineers make things work. She was the only woman in her classes. Julia did not let that hinder her.

Julia made a decision. She wanted to be an architect. Architects design buildings. They plan how they will look. She studied hard and became an architect.

Getting Started

Julia wanted to apply her ideas to real buildings. She wanted to make buildings for people to use and to enjoy.

Julia knew a woman named Mrs. Hearst. Mrs. Hearst was very rich. She asked Julia to work on a house for her.

People liked Julia's work. They wanted her to do more.

Mrs. Hearst's home

Then the big earthquake of 1906 struck San Francisco. Julia helped rebuild the city. People noticed her fine work.

People liked working with Julia because she listened to them. Julia's buildings fit with the land. They looked like they belonged. She used local wood and stones.

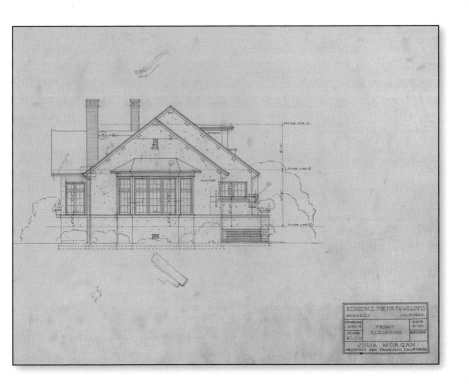

Julia worked on many kinds of buildings. She never thought a job was too small.

Work was harder in Julia's time. There were no computers. The invention of the copy machine was years away. Julia still finished many buildings. She loved to work. She was always full of ideas.

Castle Building

It was 1919. Mrs. Hearst's son, William, came to see Julia. He owned some land on a hill in San Simeon, California. His family had camped there for years. Now he wanted a house there. Julia agreed to build the house. It would become her most famous work.

Mr. Hearst said he wanted Julia to "build a little something." Soon he wanted a lot more. Mr. Hearst owned a lot of art. He wanted to show it off.

Julia made plans for the main house. It was huge. It had an indoor pool and a movie theatre!

People called it "Hearst Castle." There was a dock for boats. There was a railroad. There was even a zoo! Mr. Hearst always had new ideas for Julia. They kept on working until 1947.

Julia didn't just work on Hearst Castle. She worked on many other buildings, too.

Julia's Buildings

Julia died in 1957. She had designed over seven hundred buildings. She is considered one of America's best architects.

Julia didn't care about being famous. She cared about her buildings. She said they would speak for her long after she was gone. Many people would agree.

A design by
Julia Morgan

13

The castle that Julia built for Mr. Hearst is now a museum! It is open for visitors to come and see for themselves the amazing work that Julia Morgan did.